Fact Finders®

Life in the American Colonies

The Scoop on SCHOOL and WORK in Colonial America

by Bonnie Hinman

Consultant:
Dr. Samuel B. Hoff
Professor of History
Delaware State University
Dover, Delaware

CAPSTONE PRESS
a capstone imprint

Fact Finder Books are published by Capstone Press,
1710 Roe Crest Drive, North Mankato, Minnesota 56003.
www.capstonepub.com

 Books published by Capstone Press are manufactured with paper
containing at least 10 percent post-consumer waste.

Library of Congress Cataloging-in-Publication Data
Hinman, Bonnie.
  The scoop on school and work in colonial America / by Bonnie Hinman.
    p. cm.—(Fact finders—life in the American colonies)
  Includes bibliographical references and index.
  Summary: "Describes various educational and work opportunities in colonial America"—Provided
by publisher.
  ISBN 978-1-4296-6490-5 (hardcover)
  ISBN 978-1-4296-7986-2 (paperback)
  1. Education—United States—History—17th century—Juvenile literature. 2. Education—United
States—History—18th century—Juvenile literature. 3. Schools—United States—History—17th century—
Juvenile literature. 4. Schools—United States—History—18th century—Juvenile literature. 5. Work—
History—17th century—Juvenile literature. 6. Work—History—18th century—Juvenile literature.
7. United States—Social life and customs—To 1775—Juvenile literature. 8. United States—History—
Colonial period, ca. 1600–1775—Juvenile literature. I. Title.
LA206.H56 2012
370.973—dc23
                                                2011033661

Editorial Credits
Mandy Robbins, editor; Ashlee Suker, designer; Svetlana Zhurkin, media researcher;
  Laura Manthe, production specialist

Photo Credits
Alamy: North Wind Picture Archives, cover (middle), 7, 9, 12, 27, 29; Corbis: Bettmann, 16, 23;
Dreamstime: Extezy (pattern), throughout; Getty Images: Hulton Archive, 11; iStockphoto: Yuriy
Chaban, 13; Library of Congress, 25; Newscom: Andre Jenny Stock Connection Worldwide, 18; North
Wind Picture Archives, 15; Shutterstock: alexkar08 (linen texture), throughout, ansem, 19 (right),
Chrislofoto, 10, Douglas Freer, 24, Irina Tischenko (wood board), throughout, Juburg, 22, Lagui, 19
(left), nito, 4, photocell (wooden frame), throughout, Travel Bug, 20, 21, Viachaslau Kraskouski
(wooden planks), throughout; Wikipedia, 8

Printed in the United States of America in Stevens Point, Wisconsin.
112013   007883R

TABLE OF CONTENTS

Chapter 1

LEARNING at Home

In the early 1600s, America was a deadly place for the first colonists. Colonists built their homes out of pure wilderness. Disease, wild animals, and forces of nature threatened their lives. From the cool New England colonies to the muggy Southern colonies, colonists worked hard to get food, shelter, and clothing. School was one of the last things people thought about. In the early days of colonial America, survival came first.

In early colonial times, children did not go to school. But there was plenty for them to learn at home. Families worked together to find or grow food, care for animals, and keep house.

Children as young as 4 or 5 had work to do. They picked up wood for fires and gathered nuts and berries to eat. Children also helped with farm work.

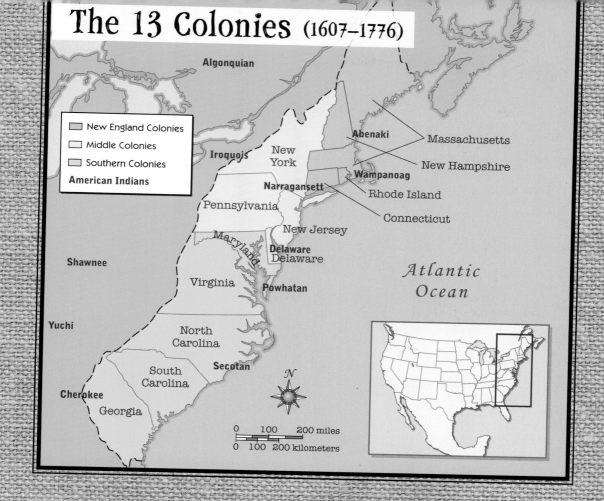

The 13 Colonies (1607–1776)

Algonquian

New England Colonies
Middle Colonies
Southern Colonies
American Indians

Abenaki — Massachusetts
— New Hampshire

Iroquois

New York

Narragansett
Wampanoag
Rhode Island
Connecticut

Pennsylvania

New Jersey

Maryland
Delaware
Delaware

Shawnee

Virginia   Powhatan

Atlantic
Ocean

Yuchi

North
Carolina

Secotan

N

Cherokee

South
Carolina

Georgia

0   100   200 miles
0 100 200 kilometers

Mothers had plenty of housework to do,
so older girls watched their younger brothers
and sisters. Girls also learned to do household
duties by watching their mothers.

SEPARATE DUTIES

Boys and girls were not expected to learn the same tasks. Girls learned early on how to help their mothers around the house. Everything had to be made by hand in the early colonial days. Girls learned to spin yarn and weave cloth. Once they had made the cloth, they sewed it into dresses, shirts, pants, aprons, and other items. Food also had to be processed and made by hand. Girls ground corn into meal, made butter from cream, and pickled fruits and vegetables. Girls also helped with the difficult job of making soap so that clothing and dishes could be washed.

Boys learned skills from their fathers. In early colonial times, most families owned small farms. Boys learned to chop down trees to clear the land. They planted and harvested corn, barley, wheat, and other crops. Boys also learned how to fish and hunt to provide their families with meat.

pickle—to preserve food in vinegar or salt water
harvest—to gather crops that are ready to be picked

Preparing food was a common task for colonial girls.

Many English colonists had never hunted before coming to America. In England hunting was a sport for wealthy landowners.

LEARNING TO READ

Even though colonists kept busy with chores, some children did receive very basic education. If a mother knew how to read, she would teach her children how as well. Colonial mothers scratched letters into the dirt floors of their homes. It was a slow process, but children eventually learned to read.

Books were expensive in colonial times. In the early days, most families only owned a copy of the Bible. Later on, many mothers taught their children with educational religious books called primers.

THE
New-England
PRIMER
Enlarged.

For the more eafy attaining the true Reading of ENGLISH.

To which is added,
The Affembly's Catechifm

PHILADELPHIA:
Printed and Sold by *B. Franklin*, and *D. Hall*, in *Market-ftreet*, 1764.

Fast Fact

In the late 1600s, *The New England Primer* became the first textbook published in the colonies.

As runs the Glass,
Man's life doth
    pass.

My book and
    Heart
Shall never part.

Job feels the rod,
Yet blesses God.

Proud Korah's
    troop
Was swallowed
    up.

The Lion bold
The Lamb doth
    hold.

The Moon gives
    light
In time of night.

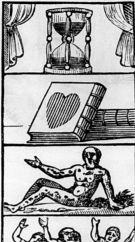

Nightingales sing
In time of spring.

The royal Oak, it
    was the tree
That saved his
    royal majesty.

Peter denies
His Lord, and cries.

Queen Esther
    comes in royal
    state,
To save the Jews
    from dismal fate.

Rachel doth mourn
For her first-born.

Samuel anoints
Whom God ap-
    points.

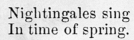
The rhymes in the *New England Primer* took many lessons from the Bible.

Rhyme Time

Colonial children didn't have books or paper. How did they learn without writing down their lessons? Rhyming! Colonial children memorized clever rhymes to help them learn. Some of the earliest educational rhymes were published in primers. But these rhymes weren't the fun playtime rhymes children learn today. Colonial rhymes often had religious meanings, and some even dealt with death. *The New England Primer* contained a rhyme for each letter of the alphabet. To learn the letter "G," children said, "As runs the glass, man's life doth pass."

Chapter 2

Colonial Kids Go To SCHOOL

As the colonies became more settled and stable, official schools were set up. The type of school colonial children went to depended on which colony they lived in.

PURITAN EDUCATION

Most New England colonists were **Puritans**. It was very important to the Puritans that each follower be able to read the Bible. The New England colonists sent their children to school to learn to read and write.

Fast Fact

Children used hornbooks to learn their ABCs. A hornbook was a small piece of wood with a printed paper tacked to it. The paper showed the ABCs and the Lord's Prayer.

Puritan—a follower of a strict religion common during the 1500s and 1600s; Puritans wanted simple church services and enforced a strict moral code

Some dame schools only served several children, while other dames were overwhelmed with children.

Some of the first New England schools were called dame schools. "Dame" was another name for woman. A dame taught neighborhood children in her home while she went about her daily chores. Parents paid a small fee for their children to attend a dame school. The dame taught children to read, write, and do simple mathematics.

NEW ENGLAND COMMON SCHOOLS

In 1647 the Massachusetts Bay Colony passed a law requiring every township with 50 families or more to hire a teacher. The other New England colonies soon passed similar laws. Unlike dames, these teachers were approved by the government to teach children.

In colonial times, most teachers were men.

The first public schools were called common schools. Parents paid a fee for their children to attend. Because Puritans valued education, common schools often took in children whose parents couldn't afford the fees.

Most common school students were boys. Girls might attend for a short while to learn basic reading and math. Advanced education was not important for girls. Most colonists believed girls only needed to be able to read the Bible. Basic math skills were needed to track household expenses.

Fast Fact

One important course taught in many colonial schools was ocean navigation. Traveling by water was common then. Knowledge of navigation could mean the difference between life and death on the high seas.

SCHOOL IN THE MIDDLE COLONIES

The Middle Colonies also opened common schools. But the Middle Colonies were different from New England. People of many different religions lived there. Because school included religious instruction, churches set up their own schools. That way each child learned about his or her particular religion. But like the schools in New England, few girls attended for very long.

OLD FIELD SCHOOLS

In the Southern Colonies, rural life made setting up schools difficult. Distances between plantations and towns stretched for miles. For many years only the children of wealthy plantation owners had any schooling. They had home tutors or were sent to boarding schools in England. Eventually Southerners did set up their own common schools. They called them old field schools. The schoolhouses were often built in worn-out tobacco fields.

plantation—a large farm where crops such as cotton and sugarcane are grown; before 1865 plantations were run by slave labor

tutor—a private teacher

Children who attended old field schools often had a long way to travel.

Most southern slave children never learned to read or write. Slave owners believed uneducated slaves were less likely to run away. In the New England and Middle colonies, some slaves learned to read and write. They helped their masters run businesses.

THE SCHOOLHOUSE

Colonial schoolhouses were nothing like today's large school buildings. They were usually small, square, wooden buildings. Some schoolhouses had packed dirt floors while others had wood floors. A stove or fireplace was the only heat. Parents took turns sending wood for the fire.

Schoolhouses had one room that held children of all ages. Sometimes students sat on backless benches lined up in rows. Other schools had shelves nailed around the schoolhouse walls. Children sat on benches pushed up to the shelves. This gave them a desk surface.

Children who misbehaved in school were often slapped with a wooden rod.

SCHOOL DAYS

School days started early with a long walk to school. Once children arrived, there was no time for fun. A teacher had to manage 20 to 30 children from ages 6 to 15. To control all of these students, teachers handed out harsh punishments for bad behavior. Students who misbehaved might get whipped or be forced to wear a cone-shaped dunce hat.

Fast Fact

In colonial times, teachers didn't have any special training. They only needed to demonstrate to government officials that they could read, write, and do basic math.

Class began with the teacher reading from the Bible and a class prayer. Then it was lesson time. Few early schools had maps or blackboards. Paper was scarce because it was so expensive. Students did their lessons on chalkboard slates or birch bark sheets. The teacher assigned letters or words for the beginners to learn. More advanced students were given passages from the Bible to read.

At noon everyone stopped for lunch. Students who lived nearby ran home to eat. Others brought lunches, such as bread with apple butter or corn bread with honey. After lunch, lessons continued until school was dismissed around 4:00 p.m.

The oldest American schoolhouse still standing is in St. Augustine, Florida. It was built in the early 1700s.

Bark from birch trees could be peeled from tree trunks in thin sheets that looked like paper.

Mission Schools

American Indians had lived in America for thousands of years before the colonists arrived. They had their own traditions, beliefs, and ways of life. But the British colonists thought the American Indians were uncivilized.

British churches and other groups sent missionaries to America. Missionaries wanted the American Indians to accept the Christian religion and the British way of life. Many of these missionaries started schools for Indian children and adults. Teachers at the mission schools taught the Indians to read and write English. The schools also provided religious instruction.

missionary—a person sent by a church or religious group to teach that group's beliefs to others

Chapter 3

Higher Education

Few students stayed in school as long as students do today. There was plenty of work to do in the colonies and not always enough people to do it. Some boys left school to become apprentices. Others worked with their families at home. Higher education was not an option for girls. They were expected to become housewives and mothers.

Actors in Williamsburg, Virginia, show what work was like in a wagon maker's shop.

This actor demonstrates the type of work a colonial gunsmith would have done.

APPRENTICESHIPS

For young men who couldn't afford college, an apprenticeship was their only form of higher education. Colonial tradesmen such as potters, shoemakers, blacksmiths, and cabinetmakers supplied colonists with basic necessities. The only way to learn a **trade** was to become an apprentice to a master craftsman.

trade—a particular job or craft, especially one that requires working with the hands or with machines

Can you imagine deciding what **career** you want by age 16? Colonial children had no choice. Teenage boys signed on as apprentices between the ages of 14 and 16.

While learning a trade, an apprentice lived and worked with his master. A place to sleep, clothes to wear, and food to eat was all the payment he received. However, an apprentice learned all of the valuable skills he would need for a particular trade.

Most apprenticeships ended at the age of 21. When an apprenticeship ended, the master craftsman gave the young man tools for his trade. A generous craftsman might also give a cash payment.

career—the type of work a person does

Apprenticeships provided young men with valuable skills while offering a tradesman cheap labor.

Entry from the journal of John Denison Hartshorn, medical apprentice:

"August, 1752– I came to live at Dr. G's. Eat nothing in 24 hours. The first meal was hasty pudding & milk, etc. Began to study anatomy."

COLLEGE EDUCATION

In colonial times wealthy young men were the only people to attend college. At first, there were no American colleges. Young men went back to England to get a **degree** from Oxford or Cambridge universities. In fact, degrees from these two schools were the only ones recognized by the British government.

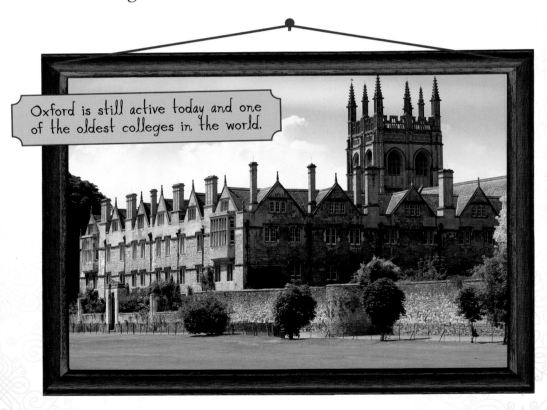

Oxford is still active today and one of the oldest colleges in the world.

degree—a title given to a person for finishing a course of study in college

Harvard University in Boston, Massachusetts, is the oldest college in America. It was founded in 1636.

University students began their studies at age 14 or 15. The first colonial universities trained young men to be ministers. However, the late colonial period marked a time of increased interest in science and education. This time period was called the enlightenment. Students wanted to learn about science, law, and business. Eventually universities taught these courses as well.

Chapter 4

The Colonial WORKFORCE

In colonial America workers could choose from many different jobs. The type of work a person did depended on where he lived and what kind of family he came from. From the timber and fishing industries in the north to southern plantations, there was no shortage of jobs to be found.

EDUCATED WORKMEN

The sons of wealthy landowners and businessmen usually attended college. These educated men often took over running the family plantation or other business. Ministers and lawyers were also college-educated men.

Fast Fact

Surprisingly, doctors did not need a college education in colonial times. Most doctors learned as apprentices. But anyone could claim to be a doctor.

TRADESMEN

Tradesmen were also called craftsmen. These men included shoemakers, tanners, metal workers, and many more trade workers. The path of an apprentice-educated craftsman began as a journeyman. Journeymen were employed by master craftsmen. After three years, a journeyman could create an example

A blacksmith formed horseshoes and tools by bending metal over hot flames.

of his best work. The leaders in his craft would review his work. If they found it acceptable, he would be allowed to set up his own shop as a master craftsman.

tanner—someone who makes animal hide into leather

WORK FOR ALL

Settling the American colonies required a lot of physical labor. The colonies supplied raw materials to factories in England. Colonists exported products such as iron, timber, wheat, fur, and tobacco to England. Any man with a strong back could find a job, even if he had no education.

The Unsung Force

In colonial times, slavery was common. Slaves were considered property. They worked tirelessly for no pay and with no hope of ever being free. Slaves worked in the fields and helped run businesses. They cared for white children, cooked for white families, and cleaned their masters' houses. Although they were not considered citizens, much of the growth of the colonies was due to their hard work.

In the mid-1700s, New York City was a busy port with thriving businesses.

Through education and hard work, colonists created a strong economy. They also developed a uniquely American identity apart from Great Britain. In the 1770s, many colonists chose to separate from Great Britain. They fought for their freedom during the Revolutionary War (1775–1783). By the end of the war, they were not colonists, but Americans.

raw material—a substance that is treated or processed and made into a useful finished product

export—to send products to another country to be sold

29

GLOSSARY

career (kuh-REER)—the type of work a person does

degree (di-GREE)—a title given to a person for finishing a course of study in college

export (EK-sport)—to send products to another country to be sold

harvest (HAR-vist)—to gather crops that are ready to be picked

missionary (MISH-uh-ner-ee)—a person sent by a church or religious group to teach that group's religion to others

pickle (PIK-uhl)—to preserve food in vinegar or salt water

plantation (plan-TAY-shuhn)—a large farm where crops are grown; before 1865, plantations were run by slave labor

Puritan (PYOOR-uh-tuhn)—a follower of a strict religion common during the 1500s and 1600s; Puritans wanted simple church services and enforced a strict moral code

raw materials (RAW muh-TIRH-ee-uhl)—a substance that is treated or processed and made into a useful finished product

rural (RUR-uhl)—an area in the countryside or outside of a city

tanner (TAN-uhr)—someone who makes animal hide into leather by soaking it in a solution of chemicals

trade (TRADE)—a particular job or craft, especially one that requires working with the hands or with machines

tutor (TOO-tur)—a private teacher

READ MORE

Hinman, Bonnie. *The Massachusetts Bay Colony: The Puritans Arrive from England.* Building America. Hockessin, Del.: Mitchell Lane Publishers, 2007.

Raum, Elizabeth. *The Dreadful, Smelly Colonies: The Disgusting Details About Life in Colonial America.* Disgusting History. Mankato, Minn.: Capstone Press, 2010.

Sherman, Patrice. *How'd They Do That In Colonial America.* How'd They Do That? Hockessin, Del.: Mitchell Lane Publishers, 2010.

INTERNET SITES

FactHound offers a safe, fun way to find Internet sites related to this book. All of the sites on FactHound have been researched by our staff.

Here's all you do:

Visit *www.facthound.com*

Type in this code: 9781429664905

 Check out projects, games and lots more at
www.capstonekids.com

INDEX

PRIMARY SOURCE BIBLIOGRAPHY

Page 23: Thompson, Catherine L. "John Denison Hartshorn: A Colonial Apprentice in "Physick" and Surgery (Boston)." *Historical Journal of Massachusetts*, Fall 2010.